A Cowboy's Life Is
Very Dangerous Work

by Malcolm McLeod

Malcolm McLeod
1889

A Cowboy's Life Is
Very Dangerous Work

The Autobiography of a Flathead
Reservation Indian Cowboy,
1870-1944

by Malcolm McLeod

edited by
Mary Adele Rogers and Robert Bigart

published by
Salish Kootenai College Press
Pablo, Montana

distributed by
University of Nebraska Press
Lincoln, Nebraska

2016

Cover illustrations: Front, Detail of Malcolm McLeod riding buffalo at Charles Allard's Wild West Show, Butte, Montana, 1893. Source: J. A. Elliott, Butte, Montana, photogapher. Photograph collection, Salish–Pend d'Oreille Culture Committee, St. Ignatius, Montana, SCC-A-0418, Albert Tellier Collection. Back, Malcolm McLeod, 1889, courtesy McLeod family.
Frontispiece: Malcolm McLeod, 1889, courtesy McLeod family.

Library of Congress Cataloging-in-Publication Data:
Names: McLeod, Malcolm, 1870-1944, author. | Rogers, Mary Adele, editor | Bigart, Robert, editor.
Title: A cowboy's lfe is very dangerous work : the autobiography of a Flathead Reservation Indian cowboy, 1870-1944 / by Malcolm McLeod ; edited by Mary Adele Rogers and Robert Bigart.
Other titles: Autobiography of a Flathead Reservation Indian cowboy, 1870-1944
Description: Pablo, Montana : Salish Kootenai College Press, [2016] | Includes index.
Identifiers: LCCN 2016006790 | ISBN 9781934594179 (pbk.)
Subjects: LCSH: McLeod, Malcolm, 1870-1944 | Flathead Indian Reservation (Mont.)--Biography. | Cowboys--Montana--Biography. | Indians of North America--Mixed descent--Montana--Biography. | Ranch life--Montana--Anecdotes. | Horses--Montana--Anecdotes. | American bison--Montana--Flathead Indian Reservation. | Allard, Charles, approximately 1855-1896. | Indians of North America--Montana--Anecdotes. | Montana--Biography.
Classification: LCC E99.S2 M35 2016 | DCC 636.2/13092--dc23
LC record available at http://lccn.loc.gov/2016006790

Distributed by University of Nebraska Press, 1111 Lincoln Mall, Lincoln, NE 68588-0630, order 1-800-755-1105, www.nebraskapress.unl.edu.

Table of Contents

Malcolm, Warren, and Eunice McLeod, Hot Springs,
Montana, 1933.

Courtesy McLeod family.

Editors' Introduction

Malcolm McLeod's particular claim to fame was being in 1893 the first person to ride a buffalo in a wild west show. The life of Malcolm McLeod (1870-1944) is a window on the world of the mixed blood cowboy in late nineteenth and early twentieth century Montana. Malcolm's story describes a life filled with hard work, adventure, and occasional danger. Through it all, he was able to survive and even prosper. When jobs as a cowboy became harder to get, he moved into trading and running pack trains to mining camps in the Pacific Northwest.

In the late nineteenth century, the Indian tribes of the Flathead Indian Reservation in western Montana expanded their herds of horses and cattle to take up some of the slack from the extinction of the wild buffalo. Livestock grazed on the open range on the reservation and were rounded up twice a year for branding and sales. Cattle and horse herds protected the economic independence of the tribes. On the Flathead Reservation, government rations were issued only to the sick, aged, and infirm, or given as temporary assistance to help new residents get established. The federal government never controlled the tribes' food supply, which significantly limited the power of the agent.

Malcolm was able to make a living and easily found work breaking horses, driving cattle to market, and general ranch work across the state. He was an example of the mobile working class strata which built the fortunes of the large cattle owners and supported many young men and some families on the reservation and elsewhere in Montana.

His work for Charles Allard, one of the cattle kings on the reservation, also gave him a role in managing the Pablo-Allard buffalo. Malcolm described how Samuel La-ta-ta-tee or Samuel Walking Coyote brought the buffalo over the mountains and started a small herd on the reservation. Charles Allard and Michel Pablo purchased the herd and it grew to play a critical role in protecting the buffalo from physical extinction. Malcolm not only rode the buffalo to entertain wild west show crowds, but he also drove them to and from the reservation and protected them like livestock.

In the early twentieth century, Malcolm took part in the U.S. government's effort to rationalize the livestock industry on the Flathead Reservation. The program sought to eliminate the trespass of cattle and horses owned by neighboring white ranchers and Indians from other reservations. A particularly large number of small ponies on the reservation were owned by Allicot and two other Indians from the Nez Perce and Umatilla Reservations. The Flathead Agency encouraged and pressured owners of large herds of small horses to sell them to make room for more cattle on the reservation range. In his autobiography, Malcolm lamented the abuse suffered by many of the horses that were sold and shipped off the reservation.

Topics Not Emphasized by Malcolm

There were a few facets of his life story which Malcolm down played in writing his memoirs. In 1907, Malcolm got married for the first time and was also convicted of forgery in a Montana state court. He pled guilty to forging the name of Joseph Morrigeau, a reservation cattleman, on a $50 check in Eureka and was sentenced to one year in prison in Deer Lodge.[1] In early March 1907, Malcolm married Mary Therriault while he was being held in the Kalispell jail. Right after the marriage, Malcolm was transferred to Deer Lodge penitentiary. He was released on February 8, 1908.[2] After his release, he built a house or "shack" on his allotment near Ronan.[3]

In spring 1910, Malcolm was charged with burglary in Polson but was acquitted.[4] At some point after 1908, Malcolm and Mary got divorced, and, in February 1911, they married again.[5]

A few months later, in September 1911, Mary sued Malcolm for divorce a second time.[6] Fortunately, Malcolm's third marriage to Lora Vine Winslow in Seattle on May 20, 1914, lasted much longer.

Background to Malcolm's Flathead Reservation Adventures

Malcolm's adventures on the Flathead Indian Reservation brought him into contact with some of the most colorful figures in turn-of-the-century reservation history. Fortunately, other historical sources help to fill out the picture.

Charles Allard, Malcolm's employer during much of the 1890s, was one of the largest cattle owners on the Flathead Reservation. Charles Allard, Sr., was born in Oregon in the middle 1850s of mixed Indian-white parentage. Charles and his father moved to Montana in 1865 where they lived and worked in various mining camps. Charles; his wife, Emerence Brown; and their three children moved to the Flathead Reservation in 1880. On August 17, 1885, Agent Peter Ronan listed Allard as having 30 horses and 700 cattle, in addition to the buffalo herd Allard owned jointly with Michel Pablo. He opened a meat market at Ravalli in 1889. In 1896, his cattle herd was estimated at between 2500 and 3000 head. Allard died in 1896 of complications from a knee injury he suffered the previous fall.[7]

Allard's wild west show toured several Montana cities in the autumn of 1893. Malcolm's buffalo riding was one of the headline events. A reporter at the Butte show wrote that

> The best feat of the afternoon was the riding of a vicious young 2-year-old [buffalo] bull by one of the cow boys. The bull was first roped and thrown by Mr. Allard and two of his assistants, after which the saddle was put on him, the ropes were loosened and the maddened beast started off with the boy clinging to the saddle with one hand and waving his hat in the air with the other. The buffalo did not do much bucking, but tore around the track like a race horse.

According to one newspaper account, "The exhibition will be opened with a buffalo hunt, after which the cowboys will lassoe, ride and drive the buffalo." Admission to the show was 50 cent for adults and 25 cents for children. One story claimed the Missoula show attracted an audience of 1,000 people. Plans were being made to exhibit the buffalo at the San Francisco Midway, but the show seems to have disbanded after the Missoula performance.[8]

After Allard died in 1896 and his half of the buffalo herd were divided up among his heirs, the family members sold most of them. Michel Pablo kept his half together until 1907 when the reservation was about to be opened up to white homesteaders ending the open range. Pablo sold his buffalo to the Canadian government and between 1907 and 1909 most were rounded up for rail shipment north.[9]

Arthur Larrivee, Malcolm's coworker and occasional antagonist, was the only surviving child of Henry Larrivee, a non-Indian, and Emily Brown Larrivee, part Pend d'Oreille, who were married in 1866. In 1885 Henry died in an accident. Billy Irvine, another reservation cattleman, was Arthur's stepfather. Arthur managed his stepfather's ranch and drove a stagecoach from Ravalli to Demersville, at the head of Flathead Lake, for his uncle, Charles Allard. During the late 1880s he supervised the semiannual cattle roundups on the Flathead Reservation.[10]

Frank R. Miles was a white promoter from Kalispell who Malcolm felt had double-crossed Charles Allard over a buffalo exhibit at the 1893 Chicago World's Fair. In 1892, Miles generated considerable publicity with his proposal to exhibit the buffalo along with a small number of Flathead Reservation Indians at the Columbia Exposition or Chicago World's Fair. On April 23, 1893, the Commissioner of Indian Affairs recommended to Flathead Agent Peter Ronan that Charles Allard and Michel Pablo exhibit the buffalo without Miles' assistance.[11] Miles' scheme for the exhibition in Chicago fell through at the last minute.[12] He was born in New Brunswick, Canada, and moved to Montana in 1878. In 1896 he was promoting a buffalo and Indian exhibit for the 1900 Paris exhibition. Possibly Miles' most infamous scheme

Malcolm McLeod in later years

Courtesy McLeod family.

was to float saw logs down the Upper Flathead River, across Flathead Lake, and down the Lower Flathead River to the Northern Pacific Railroad at Dixon, Montana. Miles insisted that the idea was practical and the rapids at the foot of Flathead Lake would only be a minor concern. During the summer of 1896, he made one shipment of logs which ran into considerable trouble, and no record has been found that Miles, or anyone else, ever tried a second shipment.[13] In 1904, he led a group of investors who applied for permission to build a dam at the foot of Flathead Lake.[14]

Malcolm died in Tacoma, Washington, on March 20, 1944. He was survived by two children from his third marriage: Eunice M. Anderson and Warren McLeod, both then living in Tacoma.[15]

Editorial Policies

Malcolm's story is published with minimal editorial alterations. The grammar and spelling have been kept as Malcolm wrote them, except in a few cases where the editors felt readers might have trouble following the document. Capitals for first words in sentences, periods, and some commas have been added. Malcolm's spelling was often phonetic, but can usually be understood. In some cases, corrections in brackets follow Malcolm's version. Malcolm's account of the 1877 Nez Perce War has the correct army generals inserted in brackets. We have dropped two paragraphs where Malcolm claims the 1890 Messiah craze among the Sioux Indians was inspired by a lady named Mesia. It actually originated with a religious messiah or prophet.

Despite some problems with dates and details of his historical accounts, Malcolm's descriptions of events he witnessed personally are corroborated by other sources. His autobiography is an engaging account of a working class life spent building the economy and community of the twentieth century Flathead Indian Reservation.

Footnotes

1. *The Inter Lake* (Kalispell, Mont.), Mar. 1, 1907, p. 5, c. 3.

2. "Married in Jail," *The Inter Lake* (Kalispell, Mont.), Mar. 8, 1907, p. 5, c. 4; *The Kalispell Bee*, Mar. 8, 1907, p. 8, c. 2; "State Prison Convict Register," Montana State Prison Records, 1879-1981, State Microfilm 36, Montana Historical Society, Helena, reel 1, page 94.

3. Mrs. Malcolm McLeod to Magor Blue, Mar. 21, 1908, Flathead Agency Papers, letters received 8NS-075-96-323, National Archives, Denver, Col.

4. "Acquitted of a Burglary Charge," *The Lake Shore Sentinel* (Polson, Mont.), Apr. 15, 1910, p. 1, c. 2.

5. "Mary Therriault in the Montana, County Marriages, 1865-1950," ancestry.com.

6. "Extreme Cruelty Charged," *The Daily Missoulian*, Sept. 21, 1911, p. 10, c. 4.

7. Robert J. Bigart, ed., *Crossroad of Cultures: Sacramental Records at St. John the Baptist Catholic Church, Frenchtown, Montana, 1866-1899* (Pablo, Mont.: Salish Kootenai College Press, 2009), pp. 188-89; *Peter Ronan, "A Great Many of Us Have Good Farms": Agent Peter Ronan Reports on the Flathead Indian Reservation, Montana, 1877-1887*, ed. Robert J. Bigart (Pablo, Mont.: Salish Kootenai College Press, 2014), p. 326; *The Weekly Missoulian*, Oct. 30, 1889, p. 4, c. 3; John Lane to Commissioner of Indian Affairs, Feb. 8, 1896, 6,433/1896, letters received, RG 75, National Archives, Washington, D.C.; "Severe Wind Storm," *The Anaconda Standard*, July 22, 1896, p. 10, c. 3; "Charles Allard Dead," *Daily Missoulian*, July 22, 1896, p. 1, c. 5-6.

8. "Looked Like Old Times," *The Anaconda Standard*, Oct. 9, 1893, p. 5, c. 1-2; *Western Democrat* (weekly) (Missoula, Mont.), Oct. 22, 1893, p. 4, c. 3; *Western Democrat* (weekly) (Missoula, Mont.), Oct. 22, 1893, p. 4, c. 2; "A New Buffalo," *The Anaconda Standard*, Nov. 1, 1893, p. 6, c. 3.

9. Bon I. Whealdon, et. al., *"I Will Be Meat for My Salish": The Buffalo and the Montana Writers Project Interviews on the Flathead Indian Reservation*, ed. Robert Bigart (Pablo and Helena, Mont.: Salish Kootenai College Press and Montana Historical Society Press, 2001), pp. 91-98.

10. U.S. Bureau of Indian Affairs, "Selected Records of the Bureau of Indian Affairs Relating to Enrollment of Indians on the Flathead Indian Reservation, 1903-08," National Archives Microfilm Publication

M1350, reel 2, frames 547-61; *The Ronan Pioneer,* May 24, 1945, p. 1, c. 2; Tom Stout, *Montana: Its Story and Biography* (Chicago: The American Historical Society, 1921), vol. 3, pp. 792-93.

11. Commissioner of Indian Affairs to Frank R. Miles, Washington, D.C., Mar. 1, 1892, letterpress vol. 7, part 1, pp. 86-87, miscellaneous, letters sent, RG 75, National Archives, Washington, D.C.; Commissioner of Indian Affairs to Ronan, Apr. 23, 1892, letterpress vol. 7, part 1, pp. 379-81, miscellaneous, letters sent, RG 75, National Archives, Washington, D.C.; H. J. Mock, "A Frontier Exhibit," *The Daily Inter Ocean* (Chicago, Ill.), June 7, 1892, p. 10, c. 1.

12. Peter Ronan, *Justice to Be Accorded to the Indians: Agent Peter Ronan Reports on the Flathead Indian Reservation, Montana, 1888-1893,* ed. Robert J. Bigart (Pablo, Mont.: Salish Kootenai College Press, 2014), pp. 379-81.

13. "Down the Flathead," *The Inter Lake* (Kalispell, Mont.), Jan. 10, 1896, p. 8, c. 4; "That Tie Contract," *The Inter Lake* (Kalispell, Mont.), Jan. 24, 1896, p. 8, c. 3-4; "Miles' Proposition," *The Call* (Kalispell, Mont.), July 9, 1896, p. 4, c. 3; *The Inter Lake* (Kalispell, Mont.), Sept. 25, 1896, p. 4, c. 2; *The Inter Lake* (Kalispell, Mont.), Oct. 2, 1896, p. 4, c. 2; *Flathead Herald-Journal* (Kalispell, Mont.), Nov. 5, 1896, p. 2, c. 1.

14. [M. A. Leeson], *History of Montana, 1739-1885* (Chicago: Warner, Beers & Company, 1885), p. 1346; "Miles' New Scheme," *The Anaconda Standard,* May 21, 1896, p. 10, c. 3; Commissioner of Indian Affairs to J. M. Dixon, Oct. 15, 1904, letterbook 709, land, pp. 140-41, letters sent, RG 75, National Archives, Washington, D.C.

15. "Malcolm McLeod, Credited with Being First Man to Ride Buffalo, Passes," *The Daily Missoulian,* Apr. 1, 1944, p. 8, c. 1-2.

The Autobiography of a Flathead Reservation Indian Cowboy, 1870-1944

by Malcolm McLeod

To my Son & Daughter
Eunice & Warren McLeod
    Your Grandfather, Donald McLeod, was born in Scotland in 1804. His mother was Irish, red headed and Freckles all over her face. His Father was a Highland Scot. He left Scotland at the age of 20. That would be in 1824. He Sighned a contract with the Hudson Bay Co for a period of 20 yrs, comeing across the Ocean to Liverpool, England. He Stayed in Canada with the Hudson bay for good many yrs as a carpenter and Ship builder and finely the Hudson bay Co got Interested in Montana Oregon and Washington. He was one of the many Hudson Bay men Sent over into Oregon Montana and Washington. He hewed out the logs for Fort Post Creek and allso for Fort Marcus and Fort OKonegon. He hewed the logs for the first Catholic Church in Stevens Co. I believe that Church Still Stands as a land mark near Kettel Falls, Wash. He met and married your Grand Mother. As near as I can come to it; it was Some wheres between 1845 and 1847, in Fort Colville, while he was Still with the Hudson Bay. But quit the Hudson Bay as soon as he got Married. Following Plaster [placer] Mineing in Montana & Or[e]gon duering the

Pioneer Creek & Yam Hill excitement near Deer Lodge now. He run a Road House and Ferry on the Missoula River, at Bear Mouth. It was Known then as the Mouth of Bear. I believe its the name of a good Size Stream, as they had to Ferry across in high Water. He finely moved back to Colville and took up Farming. He owned the land there that the Town of Colville is Built on now. He Sold that place to a Duchman by the name of Hosstter and moved up to Chewelah where I was born in 1870. Our Old Home in Chewelah is where the Sisters of Charity have a School & Hospital at the present day.

Your Grandfather Died here on the Flathead in Feb 1900 at the age of 96. He is buried at St Ignatius. Ive often wished that I had a true Story of all of his experinces while with the Hudson Bay Co. It Shure would be quite Interesting now.

Your Granmother was born in Canada in the Red River Country. Her maiden name was Roseila Morigeau. Her Father was a French Canadian. Her mother was a Chipeway Indian. The Morigeau's is one of the largest Familys on the Flathead and all of a Blood relation of ours.

Your Grandmother was a wonderful Mother. Never do I remember her laying a hand on any of us if we done any thing wrong or dident mind. She would Shame us and that was worse than a licking to me. She belonged to the Catholic Church and was a True Christian. I can remember when I was 7 or 8 yrs old. I and her would leave Home about 5 a m. and ride a horse back 20 miles to get to go to high Mass. We lost her in Nov 1880. I was not Old enough to relise what a mother love was then. She is buried near old Fort Colville.

There was 14 children in our Family only 5 of us left now. Alex is the Oldest 80 yrs old. Maggie 78. Dan 68. Me 64. Richard 60.

There is where I missed my dear Mother after She left us. I was First with my Brother, Frank, and his wife was mean to me. Would make me work all day, cutting wood and work in the Garden. Ill never forget one day a Jew by the name Minnie Openhamer asked me if I could drive two horses and harrow. I

Said Shure. I went with him on a Sunday evening. I drove that team all week draging a harrow. When Saturday come after Supper he Say's, well my boy you done fine and here is $3.00 all in 50 cts peaces. Ill Tell you I was a proued boy. I went back to my Brother's place about 1½ miles. Ill Bet I counted them 50 cts peaces a hundred times. Id Sit down on a log along the Road, and Id say, Well This one is for a Book and this one for a Hat. How I wished I had enough to get me a 22 rifel. But them days they were about 20 dollars. So I had to content my Self with a Bow and Arrows. Well I bought my Self an Arthmetic for 75 ¢, Hat $1.50, Mouth harp 50 ¢, and I guess the rest went for Candy.

I Stayed with my Brother about 1 year. Then I went to my Sister Maggie's Sos I could go to School. Them days we went to School only in winter time. We had to walk about 3 miles. But we thought it was lots of fun. We Shure had lots of fun along the Road; Both comeing and going. Well I Stayed two yrs with my Sister Maggie. Then a young Batchler by the name of Ed Burr took me. Kind of addopeded me. He had some race Horses and I was his Jockey. I was in my Glory then, for I allwas had a Horse to ride. Then my Brother Dan Seen I could ride all OK. Made me a present of a little Pinto Horse, and Say he Shure was some Horse. He was full of life and wanted to go all of the time. I thot I was Some Punkins. All the Kids of my age was Jelious of me and they allwas wanted to ride him. I was not Stingey, I would let them ride him. Well I Stayed with Ed Burr till June 1885. I was then 15 yrs Old. I and Richard and Dad come to Spokane over land from Chewelah and took the Train there to Ravalli, Montana. That was the first time that I had Seen a Steam Train, and it was Some Sport rideing on it. Both of us boys Shure had lots of fun comeing up. Seeing all Kinds of new country and every thing Just seemed wonderful.

We left Spokane about 9 AM and got into Ravalli at 10:30 PM. There was no one to meet us there. So Dad made a bed on the Depot platform. Next morning we went and had our breakfast with Mr Duncan McDonald. Dad got a team and hack from Mr McDonald and we drove over to the Mission.

My Brother Frank had left Chewelah and was working for the Sisters of Charity as boss Farmer. He did not Know that we was comeing up to Montana. So it was quite a Suprise to him when he Saw us driveing up. He had been in Montana a little over a year then. Well we visited the Coutures at Arlee and Uncel Alex Morgeau and came to Polson to see the Lake. Spent the 4th of July at the Sloan Ranch on Mud Creek. They had Horse races and foot races and a Free for all foot race for Kids from 12 to 16. I and Richard Beat them all. That made Some of them Sore. Arthur Larrive was the Same age I was. He dident run in the free for all, as he thought he was to good. He was much bigger than I was. Chas Allard told your Grand Pa that he would bet that he (Arthur) could beat me. So they Bet $5.00 and we run a 100 yds. He led me the first 25 or 30 yds about one foot. I passed him and Beat him about 10 feet. Larivee never did like me after that. He was a poor loser.

That was in 1885. That Fall Dad put Both I & Richard at the Fathers. We had to work a 1/2 day, and then go to School 1/2 a day. But was on our Prayer bones a good part of the time. I will give you our Program there Sos you can See the difreance in now days.

Arrise at 5 A.M. Kneel down Say a Short prayer, go to wash room. 5:30 go to Church. Stay in church till 6:30. When we left church we had 30 minuits recration. 7 A.M. line up for Break-fast. From 7:30 to 8:30 recration. School took up at 8:30 recess, 10:30 and So on for two yrs.

At the age of 17 I left School and went to work for A. L. Demers. He had a Store in the Mission. His Old log Bulding Still Stands Back of the Beckwith Mec-Co. I Shure liked it there. I was getting $15.00 per month. But I had to do Some hard work, Haul Hay and Saw wood by hand. Split it and carry it in the Kitchen and in the Store and across the St. to his Dwelling House. I was Kept busy from morning till late at night. But I liked it and was Satisfied, for I had my mind made up that I was going to be a Cow boy and I was Saveing my Money to buy me a

Saddle and a Horse. I worked for Mr Demers about one year. Id got me a good Saddle and I had two good Saddle Horses.

The summer of 1888 I went to Arlee and undertook a Job from an Old Indian to Break Horses to ride. I was to Break 3 head and Keep one. He had about 200 head of Horses, some very good ones. I managed to Break 20 head. I had a chum, Asbery Blodgett. I and him broke those Horses together. Any how we got 6 head of our own in about 6 weeks. We sold them to a Horse buyer for $30.00 per head. I Sent for a California Saddle, only one Sinch [cinch]. We called them center fives then. I wasent much of a rider yet. I yousto Hobbel my Stirups. But it wasent long til I could ride them without Hobbleing My Stirups. The Fall of 1888 a fellow by the name of Barney Wilkerson came to Arlee from the Bitter Root Country. He Saw me rideing and he offered me a Job to come up the Bitter Root and Break Horses and help chase Wild Horses out of the Hills. He was to pay me $30.00 per month. I stayed with him all of that Fall and Winter. We dident to much in winter, So the next Spring, while the Wild Horses were poor & weak, we Started in to chase them with good Strong Grain Fed Horses. We had very good luck. We managed to corrall about 40 head of his Horses. He had about 80 head near his place that were all Gentel. So in June 1889 we left Bitter Root with 120 head of Horses for the Milk River Country or the Bear Paw Mounteans.

He was married to one of Asbery Blogett's Sisters. So he drove the Wagon and I and a fellow by the name of Thad McAwain drove the Horses. We left Sleeping Child Creek, near Hamilton now, early one Morning and drove to the Sumit of the Mountians, 8000 feet above Sea Level. We camped at Joseph's Prarrie right on the Sumit of the Bitterroot Mts. Joseph's Prarrie was named after Cheif Joseph of the Nes-Perce Tribe. I will tell you more about Cheif Joseph as I write of this trip overland with those Horses. The next day we made the big Hole country and camped at the Battle Grounds. Cheif Joseph was a famous Nes-Perce cheif. He and his tribe Started out of the Nes-Perce Country in 1874 [1877] on a War party comeing through the

LoLo Pass and into the Bitter Root Valley. There first camp after leaveing the Bitter Root was at the Sumit of the Mts. at this
little Prarrie. So Its called Josephs Prarrie. His next Camp was
on a little creek at the Head of the Big Hole Basin. He Had all
of his Teepes across the creek on a Flat. There was lots of Willows on this creek. General Miles [Howard] & his Troops were
on his Trail following him from Idaho. They had one Skermish
on Camas Prarrie in Idaho near the Town of Cotton Wood now.
Well Miles [Gibbons] and his Troops and lots of Volenteers from
the Bitter Root Suprised him at this Camp early in the morning.
I mean His Camp at the head of Big Hole Basin.

Miles [Gibbons] Troops were all hid behind Boulders &
Trees. A young Buck had come over on Mile's side of the Creek
after some Horses and one of the Volenteers opend up on him.
Killed him instantly. That Shot Started up the Camp. In no time
a thousand Guns was working. To give you an Ide How much
Shooting was done, the Willows along this creek between the
Troops & Indians was all Just mowed off about half way up. This
was 15 yrs after this Battle that I Saw those willows and they
were nothing But dry Sticks Standing there. A cruel reminder of
what accured there. Well the result of that Battle, Joseph had all
of His young Warriors Keeping the Troops back and all the time
the Squaws were prepareing to move along, Which they finely
did. When the Squaws were well on there way, the Indian wariors
Just disapeared all at once, leaving there dead Behind. Well the
Indians made there way into Eastrn Montana and were camped
& resting in Snake Creek East of the Bear Paw mts. When General Miles once more come unto them, where they had an other
Battle. Cheif Joseph finely Surrendering to Miles. I have been on
these Battel Grounds quite often, and if you ever have the opporunity to go in Eastern Montana, I want you should visit this
Battel Ground. Its near Chinook on the Great Northern.

Well to Keep on with my Trip to Eastrn Mont with Barney
Wilkerson. Mr Wilkerson was one of the Volenteers with Miles
at the Big Hole Fight. He now lives in Missoula, and I belive he is

the only liveing white man at this day that draws a Pension From the Gov. for his Services in the Big Hole Fight.

Our next Camp was about 10 Miles this side of Anaconda. Next day, we made Dog Creek East of Deer Lodge. We rested there for two days. We left Dog Creek and Hit the N.P. line, corossed the Rockeys at Mullen Tunnel on the NP line, and camped at the foot of the Mountains on the East side. I was Breaking Horses as we went. Every day at noon, we would rope a new one or Fresh one. Throw the Saddle on him If he dident Buck Id make him Buck by rakeing him with my Spurs. After about a weeks drive from Helena, we reached the Milk River at Haver Mont. We was camped there for 3 or 4 days; and one day two Cow boys rode into our Camp. One of them was a big man Weighing about, 225. He Kind of took a likeing to me. He asked me if I would like to go on a round up.

My chance to go Punching Cows had finely come. His name was Thos Connant, But he was Known as Sleepy Tom. He was foreman for the Bear Paw Pool. They worked about 25 men. Say: may be you think I wasent tickled to get on a Big outfit like that, $40.00 per month. I told him that was my Great Desire. Allright he says, you can come over in the morning. There Home Ranch was only a $^1/_2$ mile from our Camp. Well I quit Wilkerson there. In all the 10 months I had been with him all I ever I got from him was $20.00 in Cash and a Horse. I allowed him $80.00 for that Horse. He was an odd Collered Horse, he was a Kind of red, with white Tail and mane. I called him red. He Shure become a great Pal. He Seemed to Know Just what you wanted him to do. All the boys in Camp thought lots of him. The Cook yousto call him and give him Sugar & all Kinds of Sweet Stuff. You Know on the range, we used only rope Corralls by putting the Bed Wagon & Cook Wagon about 80 or 90 feet apart, then Strech a big Rope between Both wagons. Then an other Rope from each Wagon Straight out for 80 or 90 feet. Drive a Pin or Stake in the Ground; Tie the Rope to the Stake good & tight as you can. Make a crotch stick like this $\wedge$. Get about 6 feet from the Stake. Lay the crotch down under the Rope, then raise up the crotch, and that will bring the rope up about 3 feet from the Ground. So you have a Corrall with 3 Sides. One man a Horse back can Keep the Saddle Horses in there very easy. All Horses Soon get yousto this rope, and will not go against it.

When a cow boy goes amongest the Horses to rope his Mount, he does not Swing his rope. He has his loop all ready behind him and when he gets a good opporunity to get his Horse, he will Just Pitch his rope. Some cow Boys become very good at it, and can pitch there rope 25 feet and get there Horse. If you Swing your rope, that will Scare the Horses, and they may Break the Corrall down. This red Horse I had, he got to be Such a pet around camp that as Soon as the Horses were in the corrall, he would get about the middel of one the ropes and duck his head under the Rope, and go through and for the cook Tent at once begging for Sugar. Some times in doing that, he would pull the Stake out and that would let the rope down on the Ground. Then you would See a mad Horse rangler. The Horse Rangler is the man that herds the Horses in day time. The night herder is called night Rangler. But none of the Boys would ever abuse him. I Sold red to one of the Pruitt Boys from Helena. They wanted him for there sister. I heard once that they had an offer of $500.00 for him. All I got for him was $125.00. He Shure was a pritty Horse and was a natural Singel footer.

Well I Started on that Round up. I wasent with the Round up but a Short time when I relised that a Cow boy's life was very Dangerous work. You cant tell when your Horse will Step in a bager Hole and Fall with you. Your foot may get cought in the Stirup and then your Horse may drag you to death. Thats one of resons that all Cow boys carried a 6 Shooter. Sos you could Kill your Horse of he was draging you with your foot fast to the Stirup. My first year with the Bear Paw Pool I made Chums with a little Mexican, by the name of Montgomery. I had not been with the outfit more than two months till that Chum Died in my arms. He was rideing on Old out law that morning. We had got away from Camp about 3 or 4 miles, and all at once, that Old out law Started in to fight the Bit. Apperently he dident like one of them Spade bits, and Montgomery hit him over the head with his quirt, and sayed, Oh! Dam you! That was the last word he ever Spoke. The Horse Started in Bucking and all at once he Just drawed up his Knees and turned a somer Sault throwing Montgomery on his Head and Broke his neck. I Jumped off and took him up and layed his head on my arm, asked if he was Hurt. But he never Spoke. So I seen that his neck was Broke. That Shure hurt me as I and him were great Chums. About a month after wards, the foreman told me that he would give me $10.00 extra if I would break that Same Horse. So one after noon I caught him and used Kindness with him and didnt let him buck. Insted of useing a Bridal on him I Just used my Hackamore. I Knew that he didnt like to have any thing in his mouth. In less than a month I was useing him as my Rope horse. He made an a one cut out horse. But I never did put a bit in his Mouth.

You Know when I first Started to work, Some of the boys asked me where I was from. I told them Idaho. The first day we Started out we was Seperating the Saddle Horses from the Mares. We had all the Horses in a big Carrall. I roped a big sorrel horse. He Started to buck and run. I throwed my Self down in a Sitting Position, throwed my hand that was holding the rope back of my Hip. That way you can let a horse drag you and it wont be long till his wind is Shut off by the rope and he will Stop. A Fellow by the name of Jack Harris Hollered, Stay with him Idaho! Well Idaho Stayed with me. No one Knew me by my right name. I was the Idaho Kid to all of them. You hardly ever Knew any one by there right name them days. As an exampel we had with us Arizonia, San Antone Kid, Kid Curry, Colarado Jack, Cheyene Jimmey. One guy was Fily up the creek, two Bellie, Kid Price, Chas Russell, the Famous Cow boy artist, Harmonica Pete, Kid Turnbull.

This Same Kid Turnbull thot he was a bad man. He got in Troubel in Big Sandy one night with a breed by the name of Joe Godas. This Joe Godas followed him out to the round up Camp and made him draw his Gun. But Godas was to fast for him. He Shot Turnbull thro the right Lung. We had to take him back

to Town, and they took him to Fort Benton next morning. In
about two months, he was back riding. He wouldent of taken
a Thousand Dollars for that Bullit Hole. After that he never did
like any one with Indian Blood. One night I and him was on
night heard holding about 300 head of 3 & 4 year Old Steers. It
was a twilight night with no moon. He got on the opposite side
of the Heard from where I was, took his Slicker and Shook it
at them Steers. In less than a Minuit that whole heard of Steers
Were Stampeding right towards me. All I could do was Just to
Keep a head of that Stampeding heard. If My Horse Should of
happened to Fall, I would not have been writeing about it to day.
I Stayed with the Heard. They finely quited down about 7 miles
from Camp. Turnbull pulled into to Camp, thinking that the
heard would of tramped me to death, and Scattered out, But I
was Lucky. Two or 3 days after this occured, I happend to be out
with the foreman; he Sayed, Idaho, I want you to tell me what
happend the other night. What made them Cattle Stampeded. I
dident want to tell him at first, as I was laying for an excuse to get
Turnbull. Finely he Says: I Know you Know and I want to Know.
So then I told him what Turnbull did; the next morning he payed
Turnbull off and told him the Keep off Bear Paw Range.

    Thats an other place where a 6 shooter comes in good
play. If your Horse Shuld happen to Fall you can ethier Kill your
Horse or Kill a Steer and lay down along Side of the animal in the
Opposite Derection from the way the cattle are comeing. When
they come to this object, they will Jump clear over it, and in that
way they wont be Tramping on you.

    I was one of the Lucky ones that Fall. I got a winter Job
with them. We Stayed at the Home Ranch on Milk River near
Haver, there was no Haver there then. We yousto call that place
Bull Hook. The company had the contract to furnish Beef to the
Soldiers at Ft Assinaboine. It took 8 head a week. They allso had
to Deliver 20 head a month to the Indians at Old Fort Belnap.
It was lots of Sport to see those Indians Butcher them 20 head.
Ive rode across that Flat between Haver & Ft Assinaboine when
it was 40 below zero with a North East Wind Blowing. That

Same Winter we were Holding about 300 head of Steers 10 Miles North of the Home Ranch on what they called Red Rock Cullie. I yousto ride out there once or twice a week, to See about water Holes.

One Morning I left the Ranch about 8 a m, it was Snowing a little, But no wind. I dident think it would amount to any thing. After I was out an Hour or More come up a regular Blizard from the North East. But I Kept on rideing, as I wanted to open the Water Holes for the Cattle. Along about 2 or 3 in the after noon I Knew that I was lost. Duering this time the wind had changed to the north. I Knew about how it was hitting me when it first Started. So I turned Back with the wind to my Back and East Side of me. I Kept on, But every thing looked the Same. I was dressed Warm. Just about Dark I came to a high Cut Bank about 25 or 30 feet high. By getting under this Bank I was in the Shelter, So I made up my mind to Stay there all night. I tied my Horse to Some Sage Brush and I run and walked up and down under that Bank untill morning. It was Still Blowing & Storming, I made up my mind to let my Horse go the way he pleased. About 2 or 3 in the after noon I came out on Milk River, But dident Know if I was below or above the Ranch. I rode on down the river about a mile and I come to a Point that I Knew I was about 6 Miles below the ranch, So I turned and went Back up the River. I arived at the ranch Just at Supper time. But I dident Seemed to be so Very Hungry, untill I Sat down to Eat. I took a big Stake and Spuds & Beans. I dident eat half of that till I felt Kind of Sick and dident want to Eat any more. In a Hour or So I was Just as Hungry as ever. The cook we had Knew how Id be, So he had Stuff in the oven for me. So I came out of that experience all OK.

I worked all the next Seson for the Same company that was in 1890. The Fall of 1890 while on the round up, I drank some water some whares that was full of Thyphoid Germs. We had been out about 3 weeks when I got Sick with Disentary. I kept getting worse. Every thing Id Eat would turn into Water. Finely my head ached so bad that I couldent hardly ride. We was about

60 miles from Ft Assinaboine. One night I woke up and I Saw my Mother, Just as plain as could be, Squatting right near me. And She Said: Son if you dont go and See a Doctor, you will die out here. I Sat up in bed and She disapeard. I couldent Sleep any more. It must of Been her Spirit that came and give me a warning. The next Morning, I told the Boss that I must go and See a Doctor. So I left quite early. I had red yet, I rode him to Ft Assinaboine reaching these by 4 P.M. Them days all there was was the Army Hosptial. I went there to See the Doctor. He was not in, But there was a man nurse or Stwert [steward]. I guess he Saw I looked pritty bad, So he took my Tempture. It was up to $104^3/5$. He Said, Young man you have to go to Bed at once. Well they put me to bed and I guess I went out of my head and I guess was a pritty Sick Boy. At the end of two weeks I come out of it. I asked how long I had been there, they told me two weeks. I dident belive them. Id Shaved the morning that I left Camp. My whiskers were Just Starting to come out. So I asked for a Mirror, and when I Saw my Self, I Knew, Id had Been there for all of two weeks. You Know when I was younger, I yousto here older peopple Say that when ever a civilian went to an army Hosptial, that if he happend to die, the Doctors would cut his body all up for experiment, and when I come to my Self, I yousto think of them things. I was amongst Strangers and no Kin near.

So I happend to think about a Sargent By the name of Daily. He belonged to H troop in Colville. His wife was Scotch, and come from the Same place that my Dad came from, and they yousto be great Friends. While Mr Daily was Stationed in Ft Colville, they had two Girls, and my mother had takeing care of Mrs Daily when them Girls were Born. So I asked the Stewart if he Knew Sargent Daily in H troop. He said he did. So I told him to get a word to him that there was a young man in the Hosptial that Knew him in Ft Colville, and that I would like to see him. That Same evening he come over to See me. When I told him who I was, he Just went about half wild. He Shure was Glad to See me. I told him of my fears if I happend to die. I dident Want my body all cut up. He got quite a Kick out of that by all Apperances. Well the result of that Visit, when he told his Wife about it, her and the Girls were at the Hosptial every day, and when I began to get well I had all Kinds of Goodies. When I was abel to leave the Hosptial they wouldent have me go to the Ranch. I had to Stay with them for two weeks, before they would let me Go. God Bless them. I Shure would like to see one of them Girls now. The youngest one would be my age now as I and her were born the same yr.

Well I went back on the Round up, and worked till about the first of Nov. 1890. I had about $300.00 after paying my Hosptial bill. So I came back to the Flathead. I Stayed on Mud Creek, dident do any thing all Winter. I was 20 yrs Old then. In Feb 1891 I got Married. That Marriage was only pupy Love. I only lived 3 months with her. In Apr. I went Breaking Horses for Chas Allard, and on the 1st of June I and Arthur Larrivee took 110 head of Horses for Mr Allard to North Dakota. That is I Started out with him. I quit him in Ft Assinaboine as he was Spending all of Mr Allards Money. As Soon as he would Sell a horse, he would go and blow in the money.

I went back to work for the Bear Paw Pool. I had written Mr Allard, told him I quit Art, and my reasons for quiting. He wrote me to come back and that I could have a Study Job with him for the Same wages I was getting there. So when the Round up was over, I came back to the Flat head. I had my own horses then. I came back over land. I left Ft Assinaboine on a monday along about the last of Sept. My 3rd night out Id crossed the main Range of the Rockies. There was Some Snow on the Sumit, only about 6 or 8 inches. I come down to the Head of Pioneer Creek on cadot Pass. About 3 miles from the Sumit, I found a nice place to Camp, lots of nice grass. I had a Horse I called Hunter for my Saddle Horse, and a little Gray Horse I used to pack My Bedding & etc. At night I Hobbled my Pack Horse, and I Staked Hunter to the Horn of my Saddle. The night that I crossed the Divide, and I camped on the head of Pioneer Creek.

About 3 oclock in the Morning, Hunter came to my Bed and nosed me, waking me up. He was looking down the Creek

and he'd Snort. I Soon Knew that there was Some thing wrong.
The wind was blowing up the creek, So I got up and got busy,
packed & Saddled up. I dident go down the creek more than 300
yds when I met two big Grizzlies. All I had was a Six Shooter.
As Soon as they Saw me they beat it for the Brush. I fired 3 or
4 Shots in the air to Scare them. So they took for the Brush and
dident Bother me. But thanks to Old Hunter. You never want
to Shoot a Grizzlie Bear, unless you are quite Shure that you will
Kill him. If you Should wond him, you would have a fight on
hand. They are the most dangerous bear there is. You will allwas
find them High up in the Rockies.

Hunter's act Shows what Devotion a Horse has for his mas-
ter, there fore I was allwas Kind to my Horses. Never hit a Horse
over the Head. I came to arlee that day and camped with Uncle
Alex Morgeau. I rested there a cupple days and came on the Allard Ranch and worked there 7 yrs.

I will now tell of my experiences while with Allard. My
work was to break horses and look after the Range Mares. Of
course in Haying I would help put up Hay and allso work on the
Round-ups. The year of the Wolds fair in 1893 at Chicago I had
the Opporunity to go to Chicago with a Train Load of Cattle
for Mr Allard. I Stayed in Chicago two weeks. I bought a Seson
Ticket for $10.00 that allowed you to take in any Shows and ev-
ery thing at the Fair Grounds. I was a daily Vistor to Bufflo Bill's
wild west Show. I dident think much of his cow boys, auful Poor
Ropeing. There was a 1 leged Mexican that was the Best Rider
he had. There Horses dident do the Bucking like a wild Range
Horse would.

There was a man by the name of Frank Miles from the
Bitter Root Country [who] had made Mr Allard an Offer of
$50,000.00 fifty thousand Dollars for the use of fifty head of
Bufflo's dureing the fair. He had never paid any thing down on
his Offer, But Kept putting Allard off. So about the 10 of Sept.
1893 Mr Allard recived a letter from W A Clark of Butte City
telling him that Frank Miles had went to him and tryed to Bor-
row twenty thousand dollars to go to Omaha to buy the Jones

Charles Allard's ranch, 1890s

Source: Toole Archives, Mansfield Library, University of Montana, Missoula, photo 75-6054.

Charles Allard, Sr.

Source: Photograph Archives, Montana Historical Society, Helena,
Montana, photo 940-336.

heard. There was 36 head of them Includeing a few Catalo's or half Bufflo. He told Mr Clark what he had done to Keep Mr Allard out of the Worlds fair. Miles went to the wrong man to get that Money, as Mr Allard yousto ride the Pony express for W A Clark. The result was that letter, Telling Mr Allard of what Miles was Trying to do. He told Mr Allard to proceed at once to Omaha and buy that Jones Heard, and, if he dident have the money, to Draw on his Bank in Butte City. So Mr Allard went to Chicago at once. He couldent get any Grounds to hold his exibitions and it was getting a little late in the year. So he went to Omaha and Paid Jones $18,000 for the 36 head.

He wired us to meet him in Butte City with 50 head of there heard. So we took 50 head and drove them overland to Butte. We was 7 days on the Road with them. To get through Missoula with them, we went thro about 4 a.m. before any one would be on the street. We followed close to the Rail Road and as we went by the Depot Some fellow came across the Street with a lantern. No daubt Some night Rail Road Man. He Hollerd out to me, Hay! What Kind of animals are them. I Said, a Bunch of Hogs. He Say's, You think Im Crazy, and I dont Know a Buf-flo. We Shure had Some funny experince's on that trip meeting Peopple. Horses getting Scared and Peopple too. We met two Women near Bonita. When they Saw the Bufflo, they went over a fence like two White Tails. There was an Old cabin near in that Field. They got behind that Old Cabin and would Peak around the corner. They were Shure Scared, and I dident blame them any, as its hard telling what Some of them [buffalo] would have done to a person a foot.

Well Mr Allard reached Butte the 6th day of Oct 1893. We Kept the two herds Seperated till the first exibition we gave. We had an Ide when them two Strange herds met we would See Some Great Bull fights. In fact, we had advertised to that affect. So in case that they dident fight, we was prepared to make them fight. There was only two 2 year olds that mixed a little but it dident amount to much. So Mr Allard roped an Old Bull out

THE BUFFALO ARE HERE

❧ ❧ ❧ Charles Allard has arrived in this city with his
❧ ❧ ❧ celebrated Flathead herd of Buffalo which will be
❧ ❧ ❧ ❧ on exhibition at the Race Track, Sunday, Oct. 8,
❧ ❧ ❧ from 1 to 4 p. m.   Admission: adults, 50 cents;
❧ ❧ ❧ Children, 25 cents.   .   .   .   .   .   .

The Anaconda Standard, October 8, 1893, page 6, col. 4-6.

Malcolm McLeod riding buffalo at Charles Allard's Wild West Show, Butte, Montana. 1893

Source: J. A. Elliott, Butte, Montana, photographer. Photograph collection, Salish–Pend d'Oreille Culture Committee, St. Ignatius, Montana, SCC-A-0418, Albert Tellier Collection.

of the Montana heard, and Billie Ervin [Irvine] Roped one out of the Omaha heard. We had a Big Iron ring, so we passed Both Ropes thro this ring and Started to draw them together. When they were about 3 feet apart they Shure mixed it good and Plenty, the Montana Bull getting the Best of the fight. After that was over, Mr Allard Roped a 3 yr Bull out of the Omaha herd. There had Been a man Tried to ride this Same Bull in Omaha, But he never got to get on his back, the Bull Broke down the corrall and chased every Body that he would get near to. Mr Jones had told Mr Allard about that, so on benowse [unbeknownst] to me, I Saddled him, while Billie had a rope around one of his hind feet, and Mr Allard and Larrivee had each a rope around his horns. So I got into the Saddle and Said here goes nothing! They turned him loose, he done 4 or 5 pritty hard Bucks, But I Soon Seen that I could ride him easy. So I Started to give him the Spurs. In 5 Minuits it was all over with. When I got off him, he Jumped and Kicked at me, But did not get me. That I belive was the first Wild Bufflo was ever riden. That was Oct 8, 1893, at the Old Daly Race Track in Butte City.

The next day was children's day, and I rode one Bare Back with no Saddle or rope on him. The Boys were chaseing them, like they did on the plains in Early days. I was amongest the herd Bare Back. I made Motion to Billie Ervin for him to give me his Rope, and Just as they went by the Grand Stand I roped a yearling By Both front feet, throwing it down some way or other. I got a half hich around my rist, and I drug that calf for 50 feet, before I Jumped off. I was right in amongest the whole herd and I was afraid I get Gored or Stamped on. When I Jumped, I throwed my Self down By this Calf. So the Bufflo all Devided and I come out all OK, But a Bad rist. My rist is Still on the bum from that to this day. It Shure was Some Thrill to me to ride them. We layed off a week and our next exabition was in Aconada. There one of the young Bulls got on the prod, and we finely had to Kill him. Sold his hide & head to the Montana Hotel. The Head is Mounted and is Still in the Montana Hotel in Anaconda. We next came to Deer Lodge. I rode a two yr Old

Bull there. He done the nices Bucking of any of them and Stayed with it quite longer.

It was Startng in to turn cold when we left Deer Lodge. About 3 miles out of Garrison one of the Older Bulls played out, So I Stayed be hind with him. I let him lay down for ¹/₂ Hour or So. I got on my Horse & Started him, driveing him Slowly. My feet began to get cold, So I got off my Horse and was walking, leading my Horse and useing a rope and every now & then Id give him a crack on the heels with my rope. I dident go over ¹/₄ mile. All at once I noticed, he began to look Side ways at me, & I could See by his eyes that he was getting on the Prod. So I Says to my Self, I guess I will be Safer on my Horse. So I got on my Horse. I dident go 50 yds. till all at once he wheeled around and made for me. He chased me up the Hill for 50 or 70 yds. He made two passes at my Horse, and one time his horn Just got My Horse's tail. It went up in the air. When he Seen he couldent get me, he layed down.

Well we had Several that was getting played out, So we made up our mind to pick all the weak ones, and Ship a car load of them back to Ravalli. We had to take a few head Back to where this Bull was. It took us till mid night, before we got him into the Rail Road Pens. That Same Bull when he was unloaded at Ravalli, he took down the River towards Dixon and Stayed with some Cattle there for two years. Finely James Michel, the man that herded the Bufflo for Allard, got him up as far as Round Butte, and he finely went back to the main herd. We left Garrison for Missoula where our next exabition was billed for.

There was an Old Cow in the Omaha herd, we called her bess. She was quite Gentel. We had Stayed over night at a Farmer's place near Boneta. We hadent been on the Road but a cupple Hours, when this old Cow Bess had a Calf. So I Kept the cook and Wagon Back. I waited about 20 minuits after he was born. I went to pick him up, the little Devil cocked up his little tail and Showed fight. I Shure would of like to had a picture of him, as he looked so cute. That Shows the Nature of them. I tied his little legs together, and made him a Bed in the Back end of the Wagon.

I took off one of the end Gates so Old Bess could see him. Ill Bet that Old Cow dident Keep her nose more than 4 inches away from that end gate, all the way into Missoula. Our exabition in Missoula dident amount to much, took in about 3 or 4 hundred dollars. That ended my Bufflo Rideing.

I will now tell you of the Origin of the Allard herd. There was an Indian by the name of Samuel La-ta-ta-tee had a Home at the mouth of Mission Creek, where Moise is now. Well in early days the Flatheads yousto go on there anual Bufflo Hunts on the East Side of the Rocky's. Along in the early 70th [1870s], this old Indian relised that the Bufflo were all getting Killed off for there robes. So on one of his hunts, he took two milk cows with him, to the Black feet country. His method of catching the Bufflo Calves when they found a Bufflo herd, he would run in between a cow and her calf and the calf would naturaly think he was Still running By his Mother. He would Keep running towards his camp, and finely, when the calf was played out, he would rope it, and tie its legs up, and pack it into his camp. He would Keep it Staked with raw hide Strings made from Bufflo Hides. Allwas tryed to Keep them with his two cows and his horses. Of course the calves were real young and he had to feed them cow's milk. He would allwas leave a Blanket or Some clothes near the calves So that they would get yousto the Human Smell. Well he got 4 calves that way.

He Stayed with the Blackfeet Indians that Winter, and made his last Bufflo Hunt the next Se[a]son, But dident try to capture any more calves. Well his 4 calves were yearlings then. So early in Sept, he left the Blackfeet Country, and Started back for the Flathead. Comeing back by the way of cadot [Cadotte] Pass. He had to take his time, dident make more than 15 or 20 miles a day. So thats the way he finely come to his own Home at the mouth of Mission Creek. He Kept them there till he had 18 head, then Allard & Pablo came along, and bought the 18 head from him, paying him $100.00 per head. They had to pay him all in Cash, as he would not take any checks, and it had to be all in Gold. Allard & [Pablo] had about 400 head in 1897 when Mr Allard died. Half went to the Allard Estate, and was Devided Equaly, with the widow and two Son's, Joe & Chas Jr. from his first Wife. The Widow married Andrew Stinger. It wasent long till [Charles] Conrad of Kalispell had the Widow's Share, and he held a 40,000.00 forty thousand dollar Morgage on Charlie's Share. He finely had to take them over too. He allso got Joe's Share. Conrad Sold to man by the name of Gibbons, I think in Yakima.

Pablo's Share Increased to 600 head. At the time of the Opening of the Flathead in 1910, Pablo tryed to get 10 miles Square for the Bufflo. The Goverment laughed at him. It made him Sore. The American Bison assoation was trying to Buy them, and in the mean time the Canadian Goverement got a hold of it that they were for Sale. So they Sent a representive over here, and Pablo Sold to the Canadian Goverment for $400.00 per head down to Sucking calves, Brot as much as an old one. They loaded them at Ravalli, So many to a car. They finely got all Shiped But about 60 head. They had turned so Wild and mean, that they would not turn for no Horse or man. They would Split and go in all Directions. It took the Cow boys all of a year to get all of them. They had to Build 2 miles of heavy Woven wire fence. Post 3 feet in the Ground, and 8 feet apart. The fence was 6 feet high. When they hit that fence, they had to follow it down to the River and Swim the River. When they landed on the other side of The River, they found them Selves in a high Corrall. They had Shoots [chutes] made, and made Big Crates out of 2 x 6 Lumber. Put them crates on the Running Gear of a wagon. One Crate would hold two Bufflo. That had to haul them down to Ravalli over 20 miles. They had 10 teams each with two Bufflo. That way the[y] finely got all of them. But there was quite a number Killed them Selves in fighting for there Freedom. I believe there was 6 Bulls that they never did get, Back of Hot Springs, north & west, towards the head of little Thompson. Finely they Disapeared, it was surmised that Some Hunters got them. I Know of two Hides that were sold in Spokane that must of come from there.

Well, I Stayed at the Allard Ranch till the fall of 1897. Mr Allard Died in Chicago July 7, 1897 [July 21, 1896]. I was then foreman. In 1896 I had about $800.00 Saved up. So he asked me one day, to get a hold of a place some whares, and he would give me 200 head of cows on Shares for 5 yrs. So that Fall I bought my Brother Frank out on Mud Creek. I gave him $700.00 in cash for his Holdings. Mr Allard was to give me the Cattle on the Fall Round up of 1897. So that Summer, I had Richard Stay on the place, Put in about 80 acres of wheat and Oats, and cut it all for Hay. I could allso put up about 100 tons of Wild Hay. I was prepareing to recive them Cattle in the Fall. Mr Allard had T.B. and he allso had a bad Knee, So he went to Chicago to get His Knee looked over and have it fixed up. While in the Hosptial, he cought cold. The result was that he Started in to have Hemorage of the Lungs and thats what Killed him. By him Dieing every thing went Hay wire. I couldent get the Cattle on Shares then as the Estate had to be devided up with the two sons from his first Wife and the Widow. Well the Widow got all of her Brothers on the Ranch, so the Fall of 1897 I quit the ranch. I traded the Mud Creek place to Pablo for a place on Crow Creek. Sold all our Hay to the Widow & Joe Allard for $5.00 per Ton. I got me 6 head of Big work Horses and went Loging the winter of 97 & 8. I had one Span of mares that I paid John Willis of Thompson Falls $450.00. Well I dident lay up much that Winter with my Loging, But managed to get by and had a little money in the Spring of 1898.

There was a big Gold excitement in Ft Steel, B.C. that Spring, So I took 4 of my Best Horses. I Bought 1600# of Bacon & hams from Old Man Dupuis at the Foot of the Lake. I pd him 10 c a pound for the Bacon & 12 cts. for the Hams. So I Started for Ft Steel B.C. I Bought 5000# of Oats in Kalispell, paying 80 c a hundred for it. Took that oats & Bacon & hams to the Mines in Ft Steel B.C., [and] Sold the Bacon for 45 c a pound and 60 c for hams, and $5.00 a hundred for the Oats. I cleared over $600.00 on that trip. Took me about 20 days to Make the round Trip.

Then the Klondike Excitement was on in Alaska. I came Back to Kalispell, Sold my outfit, Horses, wagon and all for $600.00. Came back on the resevation and Sold my Ranch for $1200.00 cash, and Started for the Klondike. I had $2200.00 all in cash. I went as far as Seattle. Stayed in Seattle about 1 month, then went to Portland. About the time I left Montana for Klondike there was a big excitement in Republic Wash. So Insted of going to Alaska, I came back to Republic the winter of 1898, and went in business there. Stayed there till the Spring of 1899. Made a failure. I Bought me two Race Horses, and Traveled all that Summer thro the Paluse Country, and the Nes Perce Resevation in Idaho. I finely landed in Gransville Idaho and got Jobed there. Lost Both of my Horses and all the money I had. Dident have a 2 bit peace left after the Race.

But its hard to Keep a good man down. I came over to Nes Perce City from Granesville, met Friend of mine that I had Known on the Flathead, a full Blooded Nes Perce Indian. He had me go with him to Kamigh [Kamiah], about 15 miles from Nes-Perce City. There was an Old Indian Women there that owned about 250 or 300 head of Horses and She had no one to look after them. So he got them from her for me on a third. I got 1 for every 3 colts I Brand. One out of every 3 that Id Brake. That way I got a hold of 7 or 8 head of pritty fair Horses. So in the Spring 1900 I went packing out of Granesville to Bufflo Hump mines. It took us 5 days to make a round trip and we got 6 cts a pound for packing. I went in with a fellow By the name of George Finney. He was from Calafornia. He had 18 head of mules and used Aparahoes [apishamores]. I had 6 Head of Horses and used the cross Tree Pack Saddle. Them little mules were Shure into there Jobs. While going up the Mountian to the Mines loaded, we had some very hevy timber to go thro. When ever they would go by a Tree, if they thot there pack would rub on the tree, you could See them lean away over, So's there Pack would not rub on the Trees. One day one of them, going along the Side of the Mountian, with the Clear Water River right in below us about 400 feet, he went to lean away from a Tree, lost his footing or the Ground gave away, with him. Poor thing, he Shure tryed hard to Save him Self, But he went rooling down the mountain, Pack & all, and hit the River & that was the last we Saw of Him. I think he was dead before he hit the River.

Well the mines Shut down that Summer. So I tryed to Sell Some of them Horses. I couldent give them away. I managed to Sell my Pack outfit and left there for the Blackfoot Resevation. I only Stayed there about 1 month & went to Ft MacLeod in Alberta, from there I went to Golden, B.C. on the Train. I had an uncle that lived at Windemere about 80 miles up the Columbia from Golden, so I Bought me a Cayuse Pony from some Indians. I had my Saddle with me, So I came up to Windermere, it was then in Sept.

I Stayed with my Uncle all that Fall and winter, Breaking Horses for him. In the Spring of 1901 there was quite an excitement in that Country, Both in Plaster [placer] mines & Silver and Lead. So I got me an outfit together, 4 Pack Horses and a Saddle Horse I called Kootnie. My Uncle had made me a present of him. I had to Break him to ride. Well I went to packing up into the Silkirk Mountians. There was all Kinds of englishmans coming in there from Ontario and Ottowa & quebec. Well Id get a Job Packing them and there out fits into the Mountians. After I would get them Located, so they could Prospect, I would Stay around there for two or 3 days, and I would Locate a Claim. Id take a chunck of the ore back with me to Windemere, and Show it around. Some englishman would ask me what I wanted for my Location. I never got less than $150.00 and as high as $250.00 for a Location. Then I would get a Job to move them up to the Location, takeing two or 3 days to do So, and Id do the Same thing over.

I Kept that up till along in Sept. 1901. There was a bunch of english Lords and Dukes that came from Ottowa on a hunt. My Uncle was a Guide and was well Known all thro Canada, So he had me take out these Lords & and Dukes. I Shure had lots of fun with them, But they were all good Sports. One day, as we went over a ridge, I Saw a Black Bear Eating Huckel Berries on a ridge about a half mile from where we was. We had to go down into a Canyon, and then up along the side hill, and I Knew when we got on Top we would be near that Bear. We was up about $^1/_2$ way. I was in the lead. I haled Them, and motioned for them to Stop. I Stuck my nose up and Started to Smell. So I Says to them, I Smell Bear. Shure enough, when we got on Top of the Ridge, there was the Bear. But I Knew all the time that he was there. They Killed him. So a cupple of days after that, one of them rode up along side of me and he Says, Say! Mister smell, Smell, maybe you Smell Bear. I think that englishman was on to me. So we had a good Laugh over it. Well they Shure was a good Bunch and Jolly. I was out two weeks with them. They Killed Several Deer and 3 mountian Sheep. Of course all they Kept was the Hides and heads. One of them made me a present of a 30.30 Rifle when they were allready to return to Ottowa.

Well when I came back, I was laying around doing nothing. I had a pritty good Stake, as Id Been Saveing my money. One day I was in Town rideing a Green Horse. Id Just been rideing him a few days, and he dident Know Much about the bridal. There was a Friend of mine had two big work Horses that weighed about 1800 a peace. He asked me to drive them up near the Hotel where his Wagon was. They were Shod all around, with 4 lbs Shoes. So I got on this young horse and went to drive them up and they Kept Stoping to eat Grass. So I made a rush at them to Scare them. One of them turned lose and Kicked at me with Both feet. I tryed to make my Horse doge, But he wasent Bridal wise. So I was hit on my right Knee cap, nocking it out of Socket. I Slid off my Horse and as I hit the Ground every thing turned Black and I fainted away. That Shure hurt. The boys from the Hotel Saw it and two or three run over to where I was. They Picked me up and carried me over to the Hotel. One of them Sit on me and one was holding me by my shoulders. The other was pulling my leg and the one that was sitting on me was working at my Knee cap while the other was pulling and all of a Sudden, that Knee cap Poped like a gun when it went back into Socket. Well I layed around the Hotel doing nothing, Just Hobling around for several Days.

Finely, I got so I culd ride again and I think I made Just two
more trips innto the Mountians, to Move Some Prospectors out
of there, and I got Jobed, and had to get out of there in a hurry. I
will tell how I was Jobed, and the reson. There was a Frenchman
there, had a Farm near Windermere, his Wife yousto be quite
Frendly with me, and all of my Uncle's Family. The Darn Fool
was Jelious of me and I dident Know it.

If you gave an Indian Whiskey there, and the mounted
Police found it out and you was found guilty, it ment one year
in the Pen at Kamloops B.C, and the Indian got $50.00 from
the Gold comminson for telling on you. Well this D-- Frenchman gave an Indian $50.00 and told him to get me to buy him
two quarts of whiskey. I Knew this Indian quite well, and I had
no Ide that he was the Kind that would tell on a fellow. So I got
him the whiskey, and he went Straight, to the Gold Comminson
with it and told him all about it, and left the Whiskey with him.
This Frenchmans Wife found it out at once and before they had
time to arrest me She had me wised up. That's one time that I
Shure had some pritty tough experince. Well I Kept hid, in an
Old mine, about a Mile from this Same Frenchman's place for
4 or 5 days, till She got me a lot of Grub and what I needed. I
couldent get rid of my Horses my Saddle or nothing. I had about
$650.00 six Hundred & fifty in cash with me. She found out
that the Mounted Police & Indian Police were watching all Trails
for me. So my only Chance was to get out of there on foot, and
take the Mountians for it. It was 100 miles to the Rail Road and
175 miles to the U.S. Border. So I left all of my Outfit with this
woman['s] Sister, and I never got a cent or ever heard from any
of them, only I found out She left her Husband and is now in
Washington, Some whares.

Well I took for the mountians. I was 2 days and nights
comeing about 50 miles when I hit the Kootnie River. Its quite
a large River, about the same Size of the Flathead River. I had to
get on the other Side, and I couldent cross on the Bridge as they
were watching for me there. So I came across a log along the
Shore. I worked about an hour getting that log into the water

where it would float. When I finely got in the water, and it [was] floating, I took my clothes of[f] and tied them around my neck, and got me a Pole about 10 or 12 feet Long. I Straddled that log like I would a horse Bare Back and Struck down the river. I drifted for about two miles, but Kept working it across with my Pole. I finely hit [a] Shallow Point and walked out and across the Old Kootnie River. Well I rested there. There was an Old trail down the River, and I wanted to make that Trail that night. So I made the Trail about dusk and walked the whole night. Made about 25 miles, rested all that day. About Dusk, I Struck out again. I made the Rail Road near Cran Brook Just at day light. It was Still 75 Miles to the U.S. Border. The Calves of my legs and ankel's began to Swell & hurt Some thing fearce. So I found a cold Stream about 9 A.M. I layed there all day Soaking my legs & feet in that Stream. That night I went back to the Rail Road yds in Cran Brook, and layed for a Freight Train. About 11 oclock one came along. I made it to Moye City, But I darent Stop there as I was Still in B.C. So along about 5 a.m. the Passenger came along. I dident want to Show my Self, So I beat my way on the Blind to Creston. Port Hill Idaho was Just 7 miles from Creston, So I walked from Creston to Port Hill. The next day I got a Train out of Port Hill Idaho to Bonner's Ferry, Idaho. I got me a room in Bonners ferry and dident leave that Room for a whole week, as my legs & ankels were Swelled some thing fearce. I had to have a Doctor. I left Bonners Ferry & came to Spokane and Stayed there all most all winter.

In Feb 1902, I went down to Chewelah to Visit my Sister Maggie and her boys. I want to tell you of an experience I had in the Fall of 1901 Before I left Windermere. My Uncle had Some Bear Traps out, So one day he Says, Malcolm, lets you and I & Frank, Frank was one of his sons, go look at my Traps. We rode all that day, till about 3 P M. We came to a lot of muskegs, thats Small Ponds in Swampy places. He pointed to a place, and Said, you Boys go in over there, there is a Trap there, and Ill go up on the Hill here. I have an other Trap up There. We hadent got to where the Trap was, till I could See little Trees the Size of my arm pulled out by the roots and throwed to one Side. There was a Big Buckskin Log about 4 feet in Diameter Laying North & South. It had fell across an other Smaller log laying East & west. Well I and Frank Started in to follow the Sighn that Bear had left. I came to this Smaller Log, that was laying East & West. I walked along on top of it. I had an Old Henry Rifle in my Hands. When I got to the Big Log, I Jumped on top of it & right under me that Old Bear Come up on his honches, and let a Growl out of Him. I throwed my Gun at him and Ill Bet that I Jumped 20 feet Backwards of[f] that Log. I got So D— Scared that I couldent move from where I landed. When I Jumped Uncle came along, and Said, where's your Gun. I told him the Bear had it. Both Him & his Son Shure had a good Laugh over it. He Shot the Bear & Killed it. It must of Weighed all of 500.00 lbs.

I believe that Bear Scared me out of a 2 years Groth. That was a good Joke on me. But that Old Bear Shure Suprised me. I had no Ide that he was behind that log. But he had taken the trap & log that the trap was clamped too, over on the East Side of that log and had dug himself a Hole in the Shade of that Big log where it was cool. Well to go on with my experinces. In 1902, I Stayed in Chewelah about two months, and Shure had a good time, going to dances, & Sleigh rideing.

Along in May 1902 I left Chewelah and went to Winnis [Winona] Wash. where I took a contract to Break 50 head of Horses at $5.00 per head. I Stayed there that Summer. The 4th of July 1902, they had a $50.00 purse up for best rider in Paluse City. I took two Horses with me from Winns. Mr Henderson, the Man I was Breaking Horses for, came with me. There was 3 other Guys there that was going to ride. There was nothing to it. I had a real walk away with the Prize. That made a lot of them Paluser's Sore, To have an outsider come in there and get away with the Prize. There was a Guy by the name of Henery Oaks at Colfax Wash. that was a pritty good rider. There was a lot of them thot he was better than I was. So they was to have Some Kind of a Fair in Colfax in Sept., and I told them that I would give there man a chance to ride against me at that Fair.

The Colfax Papper ran quite an article about Henry Oaks was to ride Against Jack McLeod at that fair. Every Body allwas called me Jack in the Paluse Country. How that come [about was] when I went to Winns, Mrs Henderson and the Girls wanted to Know what my name was. I told them that I dident like to tell them what it was, as it was a Fishy name. So one of them Said, what will we call you then. I told them, call me Jack or any old thing. So Jack Stayed with me.

Well when I went to Colfax for that Fair I was offerd $100.00 dollars if Id let Oaks Beat me. Some Guys wanted to bet a lot [of] money on Oaks. I told them I was not for Sale. That Id come there to out Ride Oaks. If I lost it would be on the Square. They had a Big Gray Horse from Viola, Idaho, that throwed all comers. He belonged to Wes Parmer. Mr Henderson & Mrs Henderson got up all the Money they had, and all of what I had. We Fliped a Dollar to see who would ride the Horse first. Oaks lost, so he had to ride him first. The Horse made only 3 Jumps and he Grabed the Horn of his Saddle and the[n took] a Jump. Poor Henery Met Terra Ferma. They let the Horse rest about 30 minuits. I got on him. After he had made 4 or 5 Bucks, I caught on to his way of Bucking, and I Started in to Interduce him to my Spurs & Quirt. That was one of the Best rides I ever put up. He Shure Knew his onions. He made me ride, But I never grabed for lether. That gave me a big Send off all through the Palouse Country. When I got through with Hendersons, at Wianonce, I went up to Palouse City, and went to Breaking Horses for a Man by the name of Angel. They owned the ⚡ Brand on left Shoulder. They owned Several hundred head of Horses. There Range was all thro the Big Bend Country.

You Remember where Oddesa is. We had Dinner there with Miss Peterson, the time you and I left Tacoma for Montana. Well you Remember all of that Prarie Country, well thats where there Range was. They owned a lot of Land near Palouse City. They would Bring up Horses from the Big Bend, 25 or 30 head at a time, and my Job was to Break them to ride. Well I Stayed in the Palouse Country, Breaking Horses and following the Thrashing outfits In the Fall, as I was a good Sack Sower, and Yousto to make my 5 & 6 dollars a day Sewing Sacks, untill the Spring of 1904.

I went down to Waitsburg on a rideing Contest, against a man by the name of Scoop Loyd. Well I out Rode him. A Mr Neace, who was presedent of the State Bank at Waitsburg, asked me to go to work for them. They owned 3 or 4 thousand head of Cattle. [They] held them in the Rock Creek District. They had about 20 Square miles under fence. They allso owned about a Thousand head of Horses. One of his sons, John Neace, went to Billings in Eastrn Montana, and Bought what was Known as the Baldwin Cow Ranch, on the Mussellshell River, about 90 miles North of Billings. So we put in all of the Summer & Fall of 1904 Gathering and Shipping the Cattle to Billings. Our Last Job was the Horses. We Shiped 100 head out of Sprague, Wash. I went with them Horses, and Stayed there all that Winter.

The Spring of 1905, the english Goverment was buying Horses for the Bore [Boer] War in South America [Africa]. They Bought all of the Neace's Geldings & dry mares. Just as long that a horse would lead with the Bridal Reins, he was accepted. I got a Job rideing at the turn over in Billings $5.00 per day or $30.00 a week, with your Board. You understand that Billings was the only place where the english Goverment was reciving Horses in the U.S. There was horses comeing in there every day, From all Parts of Woyoming, Montana, Idaho, Oregon & Washington. They had 25 Riders up all of the time, and had 25 men that dident do any thing else But Saddel these Horses. They had a circul made That was about ¼ mile around it, and along that circul were 4 Judges.

When you got on a horse, you had to ride by the first Judge on a Walk. About half way was an other Judge, you had to ride by him on a Trot, and by the 3rd Judge on a Loap [lope]. There is where you had to do Some rideing at times as the most of them Horses were only half Broke, and when you would tuch them up with the Spurs, to get them on a Loap, down there head would go and you would See Some Bucking. They dident care

how much a Horse bucked, as long as you could lead him by
the 4th Judge with the Bridal Reins, he would be excepted and
run innto a Shute & Branded on the neck and hoofs. The riders
dident even have to take off there Saddles. Your Saddle was takeing off, and takeing to the Saddling Pens. They had a good Size
Corrall where you first got on your horse and took the Rough off
him. Then you was let out to go before the Judges. I Seen more
than one man getting hurt there, eather by getting Kicked or
Bucked off. When ever a man got hurt, they had two men to look
after them. When Saturday nights come the Town of Billings was
nothing But Cow Boys. They were all makeing good Money, and
as the old Saying is, Money come easy, goes easy. I Know that was
the way with me.

Well that Fall of 1905, I came back to the Flathead, But
went right on through to the Okonogon Country, drove Stage
out of Oraville to Headly B.C. in 1906. That Same Fall, I got
Blood Poison in my left hand. They had to take me to Spokane,
where I Stayed all Winter. Comeing Back Home in the Spring
of 1907, and went chaseing wild Horses over on the little Bitter
Root, Had a camp at Horse Shoe Bend, above Sloans Ferry now.
A fellow By the name of Jessie Sears Bought all of an Indian's
horses. This Indian's name was al-a-cot. He was Nes-Perce. He
owned Hundrerds of Horses. But Wild as white Tails. Thats all
I done that Summer. Sears finely turned the whole thing over
to me and he left the country. Id Sold about 30 or 40 head that
Summer, had a Check made out to me, and a fellow by the name
of Jones owned Sterlings Store then. Id left that Check there with
him, and while I was out after more horses, Sears came along.
Jones told him, I had a check there for $480.00. Sears got that
Check, left me 4 head of Gentel Saddle Horses, one Saddel, and
all of the Wild Horses I Could catch with the Al-a-cot Brand. It
was getting a little late in the Fall. I cought 6 head of nice Big
Mares Back of Billie Ervins [Irvine's]. Sold them to Mr Jette for
$150.00 or $25.00 a head. I went to Kalispell to Winter.

In Feb. 1908, I Married a French Woman, a Mrs Ther-
ault [Therriault]. I lived with her two years. She yousto make

my live miserable. She was the most Jelious Person I ever met in my life. I began to feal like I wanted to Settel down and go Farming. We Tryed it on the Farm for one year, But it was no use. So I leased my land out for 3 yrs. and went back down in Washington, around Walla Walla and Pendelton Ore. That was the Spring of 1910. Well I followed my Old Bussiness breaking Horses for a while around Pendelton, and finely drifted over to the Big Hole Country. Around Dillion Mont. they had a big 4th of July celebration. Had a $50.00 purse for Best rider. I got away with that prize, and that was the last ride I ever made on exabition. I finely came back to the Flathead, and followed farming for wages, driveing Team the most of the time. When the lease run out on my place, I farmed it with Frances Dupuis, Harold's Father. Times were getting Hard on the reservation. All the range was been fenced up, and the land owned by Bankers & Store Keepers. I was getting discouraged with every thing here, I guess. I will have to go Back to Some Old History, and allso tell some more of My experiences Chaseing Wild Horses. You Have no Ide how it hurts an old lover of Horses to see what greed has done with that nobal animanl, the Wild Horse. I guess we will Just call this

Trailing along

A few years ago the big Sheep Interests, in the northwest engineered a movement to clear off all the wild horses from the Ranges. Seems like they made a pritty good Job of it from what I hear. Ownerless horses were rounded up, Trailed and railroaded out to canning plants and Sold for from one to three dollars a head. The worst of the business was the cold-blooded cruelty with which the animals were treated. They were trailed over baren hills without feed or water. Little colts, following there mothers, used to drop and die from Starvation and exhaustion. Even when loaded into railroad cars, the animals were never fed or watered and were landed at Some packing plant where no forage was provided for them on arrival. Many of the poor brutes died in the corrals whilst waiting there turn to be Slaughtered.

Of course a great many of these range horses were of no Value as they were Interbred and rundown Stock. But this was not true when applied to the real wild horses ranging over Southern Utah, northern Arizona, the Sage brush Hills of Nevada, and the high Mountain desert of Eastrn Oregon, and the rooling Hills of the Rockys in Westrn Montana. These horses were the direct descendants of the well bred animals Brought to the new world by the Spaniards and which escaped from Diffrent Stock Ranches all thro the US & Mexico to the Open Ranges and then Spred all over the west. Insted of falling off in quality a lot of these wild bands actually improved on there Parent Stock. Good well bred Stallions and mares often escaped from there owners and Joined the wild bunch and thus left their impress on their progeny.

You can See this blood plainly in hundreds of them. You can tell it by their weight and Size. The Indian Ponyies of the Plains would not average over Eight hundred pounds apiece. I have helped to corrall wild horses which would Weight from ten to twelve hundred pounds apiece. I Know Somthing about them for Ive Spent lots of my time chasing Broomtails across the Hills, and praries. As Stout-hearted as gallant as Thourougbreds in every way. Incredible as it may Seem to those who only Know the horse of civilization, I have Known wild bands to Gallop or run fifty miles at a Strech when we were relaying them with changes of riders.

They are the Smartest and most Intelligent animals on four feet. They Know there range and they Seem to Know man too. Once I remember we were hunting a big band of sorrels for a week and we finally found them circling round our camp, dodging us and only two miles away. And yet horses of this Stamp have been rounded up and butchered ruthlessly within the last few years.

Each band of horses is headed by a Stallion. He is the leader and the boss. But the Domestic affairs of the band are looked after by one, Some times two, Wise Old Mares. When the bunch moves there range one of the mares takes the lead, the Stallion

brings up the rear and Keeps the Stragglers on the move by rushing at them with bared teeth.

Whilst the Stallion is the commandant, it is the old mares
that teach the young ones in the ways of the wild and thus prepare them for the time when they must leave the herd. Especially
the young Stallions, as the leader only tolerates these as long as
they behave Themselves. By there third year, he has driven them
out of the band. Then they pick up with Stray mares and form a
band of their own.

Some of the most Picturesque phases of Westrn life are fur-
nished by the bands of Wild horses that roam over the barren
Dessert ranges, and rooling Hills of the Rockys. Exciting Stories
have been woven round these horses, but the actual truth about
them, there courage, their Sagacity, far exceed the fiction of the
Story writers.

Over in the Eastrn Montana and along the Nevada border
you can hear the lean, bronzed desert riders tell yarns of the Wild
bands of horses of Such Speed and beauty that they range with
a price on there heads. I heard of one, a palomina Stallion for
whom one rancher offered five hundred dollars. And the phanton
grays, a bunch whose capture would have ment Several hundred
dollars for the buckaroos who could have corraled them.

To Show what this work is like, let me take Some of my
own experience. On this outfit there were 6 of us and we had
7 head of Saddel horses a piece in our String. We were running
mustangs, the local term for this work, in the rooling foot hills of
the Bull Mountains, near the Mussel Shell river north of Billings
in Montana. And the Ide was to capture horses fit for breaking
and Sale and Slap a brand on the picked young Stock and the
best mares, sos they could be claimed later on.

We had two large bands, one all duns, and the other, most
all of them were pinto's, located and figured on running them
into half breed canon, a natural wild horse trap, which opened
out at the end of a long Mesa. We scouted these bands through
our Glasses for Several days and noted their rangeing habits, and
So picked the Stations where we would place our relay riders. The

day before the run, after a late Supper, these relay riders made up
a Small pack, and left for their places. One man was to drive the
cavvi (Saddle horses) up on the mesa, or you may say a peice of
tabel land flat & level and hold them there. This was for a mark
to aim at. We were going to try and run the wild horses into our
Saddle Bunch and thus make them a bit easier to handle. You
bet we Knew how to Keep those Saddlers from Breaking away
and running off with the Wild Bunch. This Method is called a
"parade" in range Spanish. Sometimes it works, but mostly, with
wild horses, it dont.

Up before dawn the next morning the boys got our Saddle
Stock up and in the corrals while I cooked Breakfast, then we
Saddled up. A Kid we called Calico Jack took the cavvi up to the
mesa. Tex, and a Guy we called Slippery, and my Self went off to
pick up the trail of the Duns, Just before Sun up we found them.
Half a mile away on top of a ridge was the Dun Stallion. Below
him, feeding up the Slope, was his band. Then they Saw us and
we heard the Shrill whistling neigh as the Stud Charged down
the Slope, herded his Mares into a compact bunch and Started
them off.

Slipry turned to the left, heading for a Snow capped ridge
which ran out under the flank of Ghost Mountain and out to the
Mesa. Topping the ridge we plunged down a Steep Shale covered
Slope So near perpendicular that our horses had to Sit down on
there tails and Slide down. Down on the flat we were Just in time
to See the wild Bunch heading up a Timbered draw. It was an
hour before we caught up to them. Then the Stallion, finding
us So close, Swung to the left and headed the band towards a
Trail that led right up the mountain. I had to head them off. But
fast though my horse was, he could not quite make it across the
boulder Splattered wash. The dun was almost at the foot of the
narrow Trail when I took my only Chance to Stop and turn him.
I Slid my Horse to a stop, drawed my colts 45 and took careful
aim. Bang, Bang the two Bullets Spattered into the Trail So close
to the Stallion's head that dust clouds Seemed to puff right up

under his nose. Up he reared, Spun around as lightly as a bird, letting out a vicious Scream, and turned back. Without Stopping in their Stride, those Wild horses Swung round, as pritty as they could. Up the draw they went, a Slim Golden filly in the lead.

After them we raced and it was Wild riding that called for Skill and nerve, over flats where melting Snow had turned the topsoil into Slippery mud, down Steep Slopes covered with loose Shale, Jumping over dead falls in the timber, Smashing hell for lether, Through belts of tall Sagebrush and Willows. No one Knows what real rideing is like untill they have ridden after wild horses over rough mountinus country with the Ground Slipp[r]y in the mud of the early Spring. Off to our right and a mile below us was the big mesa which ended in Half-breed canon. In the middel of it, clear cut and cameo Shaped, looking like of bunch of toy horses at that distance, was the parada with Jack holding them bunched. And away off to one side and quite useless to us now, were our relay men on fresh horses. That Stallion had upset our calculations. In front of us barely half a mile away, the Wild bunch Swept along. The dun Stallion in the lead again. His long black mane and tail billowing out like a Smokey cloud all around him. Then Old Slippry turned off the line and headed for a timbered Slope. He was going to ride that ridge and cut across the Stallions front and So head him off down to the mesa. The contour of the hills helped him. He Just managed to turn those Mustangs down towards the flat or Mesa. Almost in one of the draws the Stallion Sensed his danger and headed for the mountain Wilderness again.

But Tex and I closed in on him, Waving our hats and yelling like Wild comanches. The Band Stoped, whirled in their tracks, and headed down the draw. Barring accidents we had them now, And then that accident happend. Tex's horse Jumped down off a rocky Ledge, Stumbled, then upended, head over heels rooling down the Slope. I reined up for a moment, but as I Saw Tex spring to his feet and run after his horse, I turned down the draw again. When you run wild horses you have to take the falls as they come.

Half a mile down the muddy Slippry hill, I almost rode into them, Bunched up, milling amongest the rocks on the edge of the mesa. Over the edge of the rocky wall the Saddle Bunch was in plain Sight but unfortunately, the Stallion had either Winded or else Seen Jack as well as the Saddle Bunch. The wild Stud head went up as he Saw me. He Seemed to Know that there was a Trap ahead of him and with the Shure, Keen Instinct of the wild, he took the only way out. He Whinnied Sharply to his band and then with the little Golden filly close at his Side, he came Galloping up the draw with the band behind him. The Trail was the only way out of that narrow, Steeply Slopeing, boulder-Sewed draw. He was almost on me before I could take down my riata as the only hope of Stoping him. I reined my horse Squarely across the trail. With his ears laid flat along his outstretched neck, lips curled over his teeth, eyes gleaming redly, he charged Straight at me as hard and Sure as a bullet from a gun. It was only the quickness of the Hill-bred horse I was rideing that Saved me from being nocked down by his furious Charge. As it was, my horse leaped aside Just in time and the wind of the rushing horse and his band fanned as they Swept by my rearing Horse. The Hunt was over, no riders in the world can Stop the wild horses when once they break back on you. Press them to hard and you will only indanger your own Saddle horse as the wild horses will break and Scatter like the beads of a broken String.

Today the wild horse of the high mountians and Deserts is the last Symbol of the Old Wild West that the greed of Big business has left to us. Must he be exterminated Just because a few Sheep barons want to grab more of the public domain than they now have. Nature — a pritty wise Old Lady — has placed the wild horse where he is for her own Inscrutable purposes. The day may come when the world will need the clean Sound, untainted blood of the wild bands to ginger up the pampered, greenhouse breeds of civilization. For, inspite of machinery, the day of the horse is not yet done. History has a nack of repeating itself and when there time comes, as come it will, it will be horses that we shall need, not Sheep.

Ive written about the wild horses to give you an Ide how it feals to See this nobel animal Slautered, and let die from Starvation, mans best friend and helper. Never abuse a horse.

I am going to write you a little about Indian's lives in early days, as I dont want ether of my Children to be ashamed of their Indian Blood.

Indian ways in the Indian Days
Body Robes

In the Bufflo days a body robe was alwas worn by all Indians in the Winters. Very Seldom could a Trader Induce an Indian to trade off his Body robe made for his own use. In Making one, the hide of a Small cow or two year Bull was alwas Selected, carefully dressed or thined down with an adze made of bone. When Thined as much as possible with the adze, it was rubbed and thinned yet more with a Sandstone rubber. Then it was well Soaked in Brains and grease and dried. It was then washed and rewashed in many changes of water untill all of the grease had been rubbed out. When partly dried it was worked and rubbed by hand untill it became pliable. It would then be Streched out on the Ground, Flesh Side uppermost and decorated by painting a Patren of Sun-bursts, squares, and circles, Stripes or other Pattrens to Suit the owner taste. The Paint usually Black, red, and blue, was Seared in with a hot Iron. With the edges trimed smooth, it was ready to use. These robes were allwas worn with the fur inside, towards the wearer's Body. Traders were allwas trying to get these fancy robes but very Seldom did they Suceed.

The trade robes was merely fleshed, Brained, greased, washed, rubbed and trimmed. As a rule the trade robes usually feched from one dollar and a half to two dollars at the camp Grounds. They were packed in bales of 10 robes each and Shiped East. Where they sold for about Seventy dollars a bale, Sometimes more. The trader woud clear from four to six dollars on each hide.

Well Ive told you how the Indian yousto dress, before and after the whites first come out west, So now I will tell you how there war Bonnets was made. A Big fethered bonnet is Suposed by most people to be a typical part of the Indian's dress. But in the old days these elaborate and picturesque head-dresses were only worn by the horseback riding Tribes of the Plains. To make one, a Squaw would fabricate a Skullcap of hide, ornament it with rows of eagle fethers, very often fineshing the Job with a "Tail," also ornamented with fethers, silver or Small bells. An other Kind was made from the horns and hide of a Bufflo. The horns were cut off, Split Open and the Solid part hollowed out untill only a mere Shell was left. Then a Strip was cut along the back of the hide from the forehead clear along the Spine and down to the tail which was, after the bone had been removed, left on. The two horns were fastened on the hide cap with the forehead hair in between them, and horns placed from eight to ten inches apart down the narrow Strip of hide untill the tail was reached. Some of these Bufflo Bonnets had tails nine feet long. The well-Known eagle Fether head-dresses, which So many folks [think] were in common use, were not only Scarce, but were also very valuable. They were alwas hard to buy and Seldom could a Trader get one for less than two Hundred dollars.

Head dresses were for wear on formal war Parties, Tribal dances and ceremonies and visits of one tribe to an other. When not in use they were carefully packed in round band Boxes made of lightweight raw hide. These Boxes were Painted and ornamented and Painted in Briliant collars. When on a visit to an other tribe, a party of wariors would Stop a Short distance away from the encampment, dismount, arange their Hair, freshing up their paint, put on their head dresses and then enter the villiage. An Indian when in full dress alwas tyed to excite the admiration of the Indian Ladys.

Dureing war Parties a regular Signal Code was in use Both night & day. Here is how an old time Indian told me they would do at night. The Spear would be takeing off an arrow or as many arrows was needed, they chew dry Bark, and mix it with Gun Powder, then take Some Pitch and rool the end of the arrow in the Pitch. When well coated with Pitch, they would then rool the arrow in this chewed Bark & Powder. They would prepare Several arrows that way. When they would be ready for use, one Indian would take an arrow put it [in] his bow and turn it down to an other Indian whom would light it. Then he would Shoot it Straight up in the air Making a light like a falling Star. A regular Signal Code was in use. One arrow ment look out, 2 arrows danger, 3 arrows Great danger, two arrows sent up at once forward attack. In day time, they used Smoke Signals by twisting a Bunch of dry Grass together. That would make a twirling Smoke, and the[y] used a Blanket or robe to make the Signals by putting the Robe over the fire and holding the Smoke back. When takeing off the [blanket], Smoke would puff right up. That way they made their Signals, two puffs, or 3 puffs & So on, each meaning different things.

Well I guess Ive Said enough about the Indians & Wild horses, So I will continue with some more of my own life & experiences. The winter of 1913 & 14 I met your mother [Lora Vine Winslow McLeod]. How we came to meet I will let her tell you that part. I allwas tryed hard to make a home for her & her 3 children, for I did realy like her. We never did have any Serious quarrels. She yousto get mad at me when Id ask you who's boy you was, and you would Say yours. But I could never get ether one of you Kids to Say that you liked me best or Mother best. You would allwas say I like you Both the Same. We were married in Seattle on May 20, 1914, and came back to Montana in Feb. 1915. Stayed with Richard about 2 weeks, got the Cabin fixed up on my place and moved there about the first of March. In April I got a Seven Hundred dollar reimbursable loan from the Goverment. I got a nice big Span of mares. I paid $400.00 for them, got a wagon & a Milk Cow.

After I had my team about one month, I turned them lose in the Pasture. There was Some peices of edgings laying in some buck brush. The Gray mare Steped on the end of one of those edgings or Sticks. It up ended. It had a Sharp end, and entered her body between the thys. She Suffered for two days and finely died. That left me with only one horse. Well I had put in 20 acres of Wheat on Richards place on Shares. So I traded him my Share for a little Gray horse he called Tip and a Set of Harness. I guess rex will remember Tip, as many a ride he had on him. Well I recieved ony ⅓ of the crop on my own place the first yr. that I farmed. But the next yr, I Bought more Horses and farmed my place and 80 acres Joining me, giveing ⅓ for the use of the land. 16 & 17 & 18 were wonderful yrs in Montana. Every body got big crops and good prices. The Spring of 17 wheat was $2.90 per bushel. 1918 dry yrs began to hit us. The Summer of 1919 I had over 300 acres in wheat and thrashed only 1800 bus. Every thing was high, wages was from 5 to 7 dollars a day. I Seen that I would lose every thing if I Kept on, So I held a Sale, Sold all the Stock & machinery, Kept one team. That Same fall I Sold my Home. I had about $1700.00 hundred dollars left when I Settled up with the Stores & Banks.

So I Opend up a Harness & Shoe repairing Shop investing $800.00 in that. Allso had a taxia [taxi] Business as a Side line. Made pritty good. Every thing I Sold or made in the Shop was on time, and I had to pay Cash for my Stock. So the first I Knew I had four hundred dollars on my books, and dident Know as I would ever get a cent of it. I had a fellow working for me. I found out that he had a little money about $1,600.00. I went in one morning, Said, Jim what will you give me for her. He Said Invoice price. I Said get your Pencil, you Bought Something. So I got rid of the Harness & Shoe Shop, and Stayed in the Taxia Business. And finely running a daily Stage to Missoula. That finished me, broke me.

So I went to work for Pollys fixing Harness. We then moved out to the woods, and finely Built on your allotments. Put up about 3 or 4 hundred dollars of Improvements which was all Stole dureing our Stay on the Sound. I worked for Pollys till the fall of 1921, moved to Ronan & went in the Goverment Service till the fall of 1922. We moved to Yakima. Went to the coast in June 1923. You was only 18 months Old. The Fall of 1920 your mother went down to Latah for a Visit. One of Hardy's Kids Shut the door on one of your little fingers. Your finger did not get proper care and got infected. The result was that your whole little System got Poisoned. There was a large abcess formed on your neck, Just under your ear. You hadent Slept for 2 days & nights. I backed [packed] you out of the woods to Ronan, and had Dr Hidelman [John H. Heidelman] Lance it. About a cup full of matter come out. You then went to Sleep, and [I] got you Home without you wakeing up. You will carry a Scar all of your life on your neck where he lanced it.

I want to tell you of an experience I had when I was 19, that was the Same fall that I was down with thyphys fever. You Know when I was a little fellow your Gran Dad yousto tell us about the Indians and how they yousto do when they were trying to Steal Horses. They would wait till after dark, and then Scatter out in all Directions. Pritty Soon you would hear one howl like a Kiotee [coyote] and then an other would answer from Some other hill and So on all of the time. Them Kiotees were Indians, and when theyed Howl that way they were telling each other where the Horses were and how they Should proceed to Stampede them and Steal them. Well I had never forgoten those things that Dad yousto tell us....

We had a night rangler by the name of Bill Edwards. Night rangler is a man that Stays out all night with the Saddle Horses. A rumor come that about 40 Sue [Sioux] Indians had been Seen in the Bear Paw Mountians and were out to Steal Saddle horses. We had about 200 head in our round up out fit. Well when the rumor come that those Indians were in the Bear Paws our night herder quit. So no one would take the Horses out at night. Finely Tom came to me and said, Idaho, if you will take the night heard, there is $75.00 a month in it. I told him that Id take them out.

One night after I had been hearding for about a week, I heard Kiotees Howling and answering each other from diffrent directions. Right away I thot of what Dad yousto tell us Kids. I went around the Horses and Bunched them up a little closer together. He yousto tell us how one or two Indians would crawl up on there hands & Knees, or Stomach, then Stampede the herd. As I Said I went around the Horses twice. The Second time around Id a Swore I Seen an Indian crawling up towards the Horses. Jee's I felt my hair raise up. I Kept on getting the horses to gether and headed them twords camp wich was about ½ a mile away. By that time I Kind of cooled off and made up my mind to go back and Shoot up Mr Indian. I went Back towards where Id Seen him and Id a Swore that he had crawled about 100 yds closer. So I Spoke 3 times, asked who was there, and got no answer. So I fired 3 Shots, and I thought I Saw that Indian legs Kicking up in the air. 3 Shots is allso a Signal for help. We allwas Kept 6 or 8 head of Horses Saddled ready for any thing like that in Camp. After I Shot I got in behind the Horses & was makeing for camp. When I met the forman & 3 more of the boys, we got the horses in the rope corral.

So Tom Said lets go Back and See. We may find a whole Bunch of Indians. Well we went Straight to where I Shot at the Indian. When we was about 30 feet away yet, the Boss Says I guess the Kid has got an Indian. Well we all rode up. There was no Indian there. But 3 bunches of Sage brush. It was a twilight night. We all went back to where I was when I Shot, and they all Said it Shure looked like a person laying on his Bellie. Well, that was a Joke on me. Amongst some of the boys, they called me the Sage brush Kid for quite a while. They wouldent Joke me around Tom, for he told them that I was nothing But a Kid and wasent affraid to take the night heard, where that none of them wanted to go out with the herd....

You Both Know about my experiences in and around Tacoma So I will not Say any thing about that, only Ive often wished that my helth would have been So that I could of Stayed in Tacoma, as I Shure liked the Puget Sound, and I liked the peopple around there. If it wasent for you two Children Id call my life a wasted life. When I was Singel, I allwas thot that if ever I married to Settle down all I wanted was a boy & Girl. Seems like that my wish was granted, and you two are all the happyness I have on earth. To Say that my life has been a happy one, it never was. Perhas if my mother hadent died while I was young, my life

might of been a diffrent life. But I guess I have no one to blame
But my Self.

I guess a body makes his or hers own Hell. Perhaps if Id
had foresight enough I wouldent be in the circumstances that I
am in to day. We alwas made good money and Spent it Freely,
and nothing done my heart more good then when Id meet Some
poor person in hard circumstances, to help them by giveing them
a few dollars. But very few that Ive met and helped, that ever did
appreciate it. Peopple now days are not like they yousto be 40 yrs
ago, your word then was your Bond.

I will close this now and perhaps Some day you may want
to ad Some thing on to it. My Sincere wish is that eather [nei-
ther] one of my Children will go thro the unhappy life that Ive
went thro. Of course there are lots of things that I have done and
went thro, that I think it wouldent do for me to put in writeing.
If I was rid of my asthma I feal as though I would be good for 20
yrs yet. But in the condition I am, I can never tell when I will be
called to the last round up across the big devide.

Index

Thank You

We would like to thank the McLeod family for their help with this publication and for giving us permission to publish Malcolm's autobiography and accompanying photographs.

Hopefully this resulting book reflects well your pride in his life and accomplishments.

Thanks also to Corky Clairmont of Pablo, Montana, for the cover design.

The Editors

Malcolm and Warren McLeod, Blue Bay, Flathead Lake,
Montana, 1939.

Courtesy McLeod family.